Shrimadh Sreeraj is a young writer of ten years' old who loves literature. She is extremely enthusiastic to listen and observe the nature and surroundings to develop her imagination for writing poems. She is **an Award winner of 29th cycle of the "Prestigious Educational Excellence Award for Distinguished Students" by Sharjah Government in 2022-23.**

Shrimadh Sreeraj, a grade 5 student at Ambassador School Sharjah, UAE, at a tender age of nine, her passion towards literature and writing was noted. Her first book 'Joy of Small Things', ten short stories of her early childhood memories was published in 2023. It was taken to heart by readers and reviewers of different age groups. Her parents are her main motivating factor. They provided all avenues for their child to master her passion.

Besides creative writing, Shrimadh too appreciates the fascinating colors of nature and its fabulous hues and blends to create paintings with diverse innovative skills. Her artistic skills have created opportunities to participate and win in various inter-school level art competitions. Furthermore, she has acquired a strong foundation in linguistic skills mainly in English, Arabic, French and Malayalam languages by achieving good positions in international and inter-school competitions, namely in poem versification and recitation, speaking, news reading, advertisement and broadcasting. She has also won meritorious scores in international competitive exams like SPELLBEE Global UK, French DELF Prime, IBT Arabic and Math Olympiad.

Shrimadh Sreeraj has been a guest speaker in All India Radio, Thrissur and Kochi FM stations and she has been a motivational speaker in schools, mainly to inspire and develop students in their reading and writing skills. Besides, her academic excellence, Shrimadh's keen interest and passion towards dance, has turned her into a talented Indian classical dancer. She is truly a student admired by all for her positivity and perseverance in all her undertakings.

English Language
Iridescent Bubbles
(Poems)
by
Shrimadh Sreeraj

♦

Published in November 2024
by Kairali Books Private Limited
Thalikkavu Road, Kannur.
Ph : 0497-2761200
E-Mail : kairalibooksknr@gmail.com

♦

Cover Painting & Illustrations
Shrimadh Sreeraj & Dr Sajini Subrahmanian

♦

91/24-25/Sl.No.1658/150/NS.18.6
ISBN 978-93-5973-235-0

IRIDESCENT BUBBLES

Shrimadh Sreeraj

Kairali Books

DEDICATION

My first book of poems **"IRIDESCENT BUBBLES"** took its form after much deliberation, reflection and consideration on how to merge apt choices of diction to my flow of thoughts, in order to engross my readers to visualise the settings as they enjoy the messages in my poems.

I dedicate my first book of poems **"IRIDESCENT BUBBLES"** to my beloved English teacher, **Ms Rebecca Louis** at Ambassador School Sharjah, UAE, who inspired me to take the pleasure and get delighted in the mesmerising and captivating beauty of poetry.

To my beloved parents, **Mr. Sreeraj Sudersanan and Dr. Sajini Subrahmanian,** I sincerely appreciate their understanding, encouragement and the support they rendered, while these poems were being written, especially when I indulge in scribbling my ideas, which most often sprouts at odd times of the day.

My thought, too goes to all those who have been a part and parcel in this amazing journey of mine.

THANK YOU ALL.

SHRIMADH SREERAJ

PREFACE

I have reflected on myself and I have always felt that I have a tendency of visualising and contemplating about people, scenarios, things and the multitude modes of emotions and impressions they evoke in me. These thoughts come very quick and they vanish too soon. But to me, those are truly astonishing and momentous thoughts I treasure.

Each time when I ponder on the same thought, I am surprised by the different feelings and the dimensions that emerged. It was such a pleasure to write it down in my diary and gather them into this book title **"IRIDESCENT BUBBLES"**.

I am grateful to Dr Girija Kumari Nair and Dr Shoba Joe for their valuable guidance and close scrutiny. I hope all of you, my beloved readers, can feel and enjoy my thoughts that are like iridescent bubbles which will pop within seconds and can be viewed in a variety of colours from different angles.

Shrimadh Sreeraj
shrimadhsajsree@gmail.com
Sharjah, UAE, 2024

FOREWORD

When Shrimadh's mother, Dr. Sajini, approached me to write this foreword, I initially felt uncertain. Could I truly relate to the world of a 10-year-old child, especially one growing up in a bustling metropolitan city, surrounded by the advancements of a new technological era? My own childhood, spent in a quiet village nearly four decades ago, seemed worlds apart from hers. With that hesitation in mind, I began reading her poem. But to my surprise, it didn't take long for my doubts to dissolve. I couldn't quite tell if she had drawn me back into my own childhood, or if her perspective had already achieved the depth of an adult's. Creativity, after all, has a way of transcending both time and space.

With Iris, rainbows invited me into her enchanting world. Not only did childhood butterflies flutter around me once more, but I was also struck by the sad realisation that I am yet to rediscover the fireflies I left behind in my younger days. Her words transported me to the quiet corners of my childhood, where books were my only companions-where I not only read but could see the magical illustrations and even smell the pages of those cherished fairy tales. As she writes, "No more dullness from now on, whether it's day or night." I found myself once again in that world of fantasy, a place I always long to return to. Yes, she could take me to a cosy place where there are no rules at all-" ready to rock, sing, dance, and dream!" with her!

May your words continue to blossom dear Shrimadh, and may your poetic journey lead you to ever-greater heights of creativity and inspiration. Wishing you all the best as you grow into the remarkable poet you're destined to become!

Cina K S
Writer, Artist, Animation VFX professional

Contents

Iris the Messenger
of Gods

Iris, the messenger
Her twinkling blue eyes
A treat to the mind indeed...
Her rosy red lips
The colour of a bloomed red rose!

Her soft chubby cheeks!
So pink and bouncy they are
Her smile, bright as the sun
Lighting up a thousand lamps
In the darkest of nights....

Her brown hair
As silky as the green grass,
And as fluffy as the clouds....
Her voice
A rhythmic melody
For the ears ever so sweet
Is her lovely voice....

Her rainbow coloured gown,
Full of glitters!
Golden and silver sparks
Making her shine like a star

When she slides over the rainbow
At daylight,
A flurry of magnificent butterflies
Surrounds her...
At dusk,
A glow of fireflies joins her

Why does Iris have such a magical power??
Because,
She sustains peace and harmony
By connecting God to mortals

Truly a magical power
That children hold anew
The innocence of children
The secret magical power indeed

Every child
Has an Iris in them,
Who brings heaven to Earth....!

My Mysterious
Friend

My home,
A wondrous place indeed….
Joyful and buzzing night life
But day life…… Dull!
Looking through the window
All day long….

Can't bear, parents at work
Home alone!
Nobody to talk and share
Everything so still….

Bored of the regular routine,
A pleasant change, very much needed.
More than I had expected!
The world of spellbinding books
Awaited beckoning to me
What a great surprise!

So plain was my home
During daylight
But now filled with books
For my glee….
Chapter to chapter…
Page to page

Marvellous poems and spectacular stories,
My best friends
No more dullness from now on
Whether it's day or night.

A Funny Crazy Day

Oh, it is a sunny and rainy day
But wait ... how is that possible?
Yes! It is a sunny and rainy day.

A glittery rainbow on the way!
Children are really enthusiastic!
Because they can jump in puddles.

The pitter-patter rain pouring down
Oh, how they love the rain!
How wonderful it is!
To see the plants dancing in the rain
They must be happy
Because they can grow more and more.

But just think about our grandmothers...
They are disappointed
Because, they can't dry papads in the sun
Making papads was their diligence though

All of a sudden,
The rain fades away
The golden sun shines bright
With all its might!

Now grandmothers are enthusiastic
To dry the papads
Also the perfect time for children
To enjoy a delicious ice cream

Oh, it's such a lovely day....!
A beautiful sunny **and** rainy day!

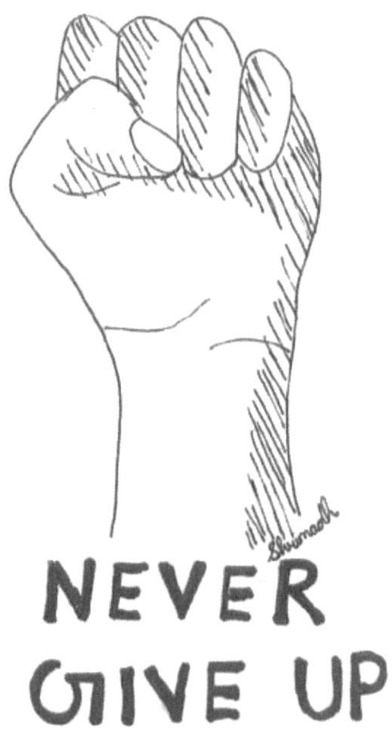

Never Give up

If you can't do something
Never give up!
Instead,
Boost yourself up

 Keep your mind set
You are the best of yourself
Also born to do it
Beyond question.

When you give up,
You have no control
On yourselves
Dropping confidence all way long…

If you're turning away, from your goal
Then you might be
Blowing the candle of hope
In the darkroom of obstacles….

You are disrespecting yourselves
And hurting the true self of your soul
The guiltier you'll feel
The more depressed you will go

If you never give up
And ought to be determinate
Undoubtedly, the startling rewards
Will be gifted to you.

I have a message for all
'Be strong'
'Be brave'
'Be confident'

Life Journey of a
little Seed

Me, being a little seed
Sleeping in the cosy cradle
Of warm soil
For a long time, I guess

I woke up by the touch of a cold finger
It was a tributary of water though
Which lifted me from
My homey soil blanket

The gentle breeze whispered
'It's time for you to open your eyes'
A surprise for me, truly
The Golden and Mighty Sun

Fluttering butterflies, buzzing bees
And glittery rainbows in the daylight,
Glistening fireflies in the moonlight,
Made me astonished!

My green arms grew,
And tightly hugged my mother earth
With my wide spread roots,
I felt proud being a sapling!

Slowly, nature moulded me,
To a matured plant
Bearing flowers and fruits
Spreading happiness and joy to all

Let my future generation
Flourish like never before.

Health and
Wealth Rules

Feeling bored and gloomy today
Cause, I'm sick and can't go to my favourite place
My school
Going to school was my diligence though

Meeting friends and tutors were real fun
But the School Bus Nanny's thermometer turned RED!
Had to abide
The 'Stay Home if Unwell' policy of my school

If I was not ill,
By now, I would've been in my amazing school
The morning terror will come as usual!
No escape from the PE teachers' 'Regular Hygiene Check'

When moving from mysteries of math
To surprises of science
'Brain breaks' are on the way
To chillax us a bit…!

We're extremely enthusiastic
When we hear the 'Water Bell….'
Which quenches our thirst
 And parents' worrying thoughts of dehydration.

We rock the 'Regular Breaks'
Garnishing healthy food with chit chats and laughter
To confirm the physical fitness, here comes
Miss Performing Arts & Mr Physical Education

My school's strict rules
Will make us healthy, happy
And role models to others
Oh, how wonderful and caring my school is!

Thought Bubbles

At the start of the day,
I'm feeling good
Having fun
Playing with friends at the babysitting centre.

But, thinking about mom
Thinking about dad
Isolated and lonely, it makes me feel

The red circles on the calendar
Representing overtime duty dates
I just hate
Cause, I will be isolated
From parents and home

Sometimes, I feel like crying
Cause, I want to be at home
Enjoying with my parents
Every tiny second.

Scent of my mother's office clothes
Eager, it makes me
Sound of my father's car key clinking
They are back to pick me

Running to the doorstep
To welcome my parents
Truly my heavenly pleasure….

A journey of life

The journey of life
Sometimes interesting
Often dull
But we have to face it all.

We meet distinct people
In this journey
Some caring and loving
While others filled with envy.

We open our eyes and start our journey,
We see the world around us
As infants
So cheerful we are.

As we go from station to station,
As children
Facing small difficulties
Along the way.

When we grow,
Our emotions also develop
As a teenager
We shan't be low.

We choose a partner in life
To have a family.
With whom we can communicate
Without any limits.

As we grow,
We get lessons from experiences
Which teach us
And we become a great element for others.

We hold the hands of our partner
And take every step
And enjoy life!

When we feel,
The journey of life is about to end
We remember the amazing journey, smile
And slowly leave for the heavenly abode,
Coming to the end of the journey...

Gaming Addiction

Every generation
Something's invented
Popular it becomes
Addicting people all way along

Exactly,
Video games, online games and more
A colossal obsession indeed
Leading the wrong track

The exotic number of video games
Might be distancing young gamers
From the love and warmth of family

Locked up
In world of competitions and cruelty
Surrounding them
Are evil addictions...

Distancing themselves
From nature and bonds
No rooms for creativity and imagination
But just competition spirit alone....
Our abilities withering
Isolated and lonely
It makes us feel.

Mother Earth

In our busy lifestyles,
No one thinks about
Who is helping us
The most!

Absolutely right you are,
It's our Mother Earth
Because of her,
We are here!

Mother Earth,
Supporting us in every way
But we're harming her to extinction

Our eyes covered with the greedy thoughts
Sadly, not thinking of life
Cutting trees
And harming earth

Using plastic all year long
Knowing the consequence but ain't thinking
About it
The factories
Releasing toxic gasses
And plastic waste too
Won't decompose too....

Mother Earth
Continuing to help us
Even when we're harming her,
She is truly a MOTHER for all...

She isn't able to breathe
Cause, your mind has stuck on to money
Then your mother won't be alive

When Mother Earth
Just cannot bear it
Natural calamities happen
As a caution sign
'SAVE ME MY DEAR CHILDREN'

Not able to control herself
Starts trembling with fear
About her children's future
Making us experience earthquakes

Sometimes, breaks down crying
Because of the pain
Mother faces
Creating floods and havoc
Leading to tsunamis too....

Her Mind,
Shatters with sorrow indeed
Engendering land slides
Causing people to suffer

Her heart burning
Volcanoes erupt
It's like her mind is on fire
Thinking her fate
Where plastic found ruling the world

Even when this is happening
Why are your eyes not opening?
Still locked up in the room of greedy thoughts
On 'Money'

Please, Wake up!
Wake up from your slumber of greediness for wealth
Your Mother is awaiting you
With tears flowing like rivers
And a heart that's beating fast for you....

Mother Earth says
"The pains of a Mother you will never know"
"I continued to support you and shall do the same"
"But, will someone hear me?"

Sisterhood

When I walk,
Through the crowded ground of my school
Sad the most
It makes me feel.

My friends holding their sister's hands
Dropping them in their classes
"Bye Brother! See you in the afternoon!"
"Have a good day at school sister"
The voices I hear

Why can't I have?
Wish to have too
A sister for sure
The most I shall take care of her

Treating my friends' sisters
Just like my own
Offering more love
To make me forget of my sorrow indeed

Holding their hands
Their little cute smile
A colossal relief truly
In the large courtyard of my busy mind

I dreamt every night
A white stork carrying a sac
With a baby girl inside
Though it never happened

The long-awaited desire
For sisterhood
Driven me to tell
Fake stories about my cutie pie

I tell my friends
'The wondering stories of my sister'
The bond of love between us
Which astonishes my friends

"I take my sister to the park everyday"
"I share all my things indeed with her"
"Oh wow…." Says my friends.
Our conversations continuing wonderfully

But nobody knows
And no one will know for sure
Until dusk ends and dawn rises
It was all a lie
It was just my baby doll.

Fairy Tales

Mesmerises me
Are what fairy tales do
Take me and you to the world out there
The World of Imagination

Beautiful ladies with flowers on their head
The fragrance of them aromatic
Walking by the lake
In the enchanted forest

When night falls,
The queen fairy takes a tour through
The enchanted forest
With fireflies leading her way
Guarding her as brave soldiers

Fairy tales
Truly a magic power
It can change your life anew

An interesting ingredient too
To experiment with
For little children like me...
Connecting stories and poems to their minds

Fairy tales being,
The only key,
May be for the locked door
In which 'The gem of Imagination' beholds.

Failures
Vs
Victories

"Hello! Myself Joyful Victory"
Says Joyful Victory.
"Oh the one, whom everyone loves"
Says Grumpy Failure.

Oh Grumpy Failure,
How gloomy he is!
Oh, and here comes Joyful Victory
She claims for sure
She spreads happiness.

"I'm the one who's important,
spreading happiness to the world"
Madame Victory declares herself.

"No, you aren't!"
Replies Grumpy Failure.
I create resilience,
The skill of not giving up.
Said our grumpy friend.

"I encourage all," said Joyful Victory
She said, regaining her prowess
Going on unstoppably
Was their grand argument.

A girl was walking by
Hearing the conversation
She stopped by
To advise them.

She said,
"You both shan't argue anymore,"
Joyful Victory and Grumpy Failure,
"You both are important".

"Never be sad," Grumpy Failure
You create humility in beings
Victory helps you encourage yourself
while failures teach you lessons.

"You both shan't fight"
You both are essential for the world.
I assure, I assure.

Cosy Place

A cosy and warm place it is,
Filled with the warmth of stories
That we can listen
Till we flow into the world of dreams.

A whole universe indeed
Full of mysteries, secrets, surprises,
Fairies, dragons, beanstalks,
And princesses too,
No boundaries for anything too.

No compulsion for food
Treated like kings and queens
Away from scolding
With round big eyes looking stern.

A peaceful place
Like relaxing in the beach
No pressure for homework
Rest assured.

Comfortable in books, drawing
And stories
Dug up in books
Truly stories indeed
Swallowing me up.

What about hardened rules?
No such rules at all!
Isn't that great?

Free to share everything
Without restriction to topics
Free for all activities, they are
They shan't say,
 "I have work, we'll play later".

Ready to rock
Sing, dance and dream
Their dreams are like
Our bestie's desires

It's none other than
My grandparents' home.

Teachers
to the world

Dear Teachers...
You are like the Trees
Who provide us shades and fruits
You are the reason for our breath
Who make us upright and firm

Dear Teachers...
You are like the Ocean
Deep and great
Make us blissful
With pearls of wisdom and good deeds.
You absorb all our bad things
And make us into good inhabitants of earth

Dear Teachers...
You are like the Wind
Fierce and calming at the same time.
You spread the fragrance of moral values
Through us to the world.

Dear Teachers...
You are like the Sun
The source of life
You are the fount of inspiration
You mould us for the future of the country.